STANDING IN THE GAP

DR. JOSEPH A. SEYMOUR

Atria Book Publishing
USA

Atria Book Publishing

USA

ISBN: 978-1-61240-008-2

First Edition

First published by Atria Book Publishing

September 2011

Printed in the United States of America.

DEDICATION

Dedicated to my mother and father who raised me in the admonition of the Lord.

Love, your son Joe.

CONTENTS

FORWARD

I first met Joe Seymour during a tent revival in Ohio. He was playing a Hammond B-3 organ. Never in my life had I ever heard such wonderful music emanate from a musical instrument! His fingers glided over the ivory keys like lightning and anointing seemed to pour from the Leslie speakers. One moment soft, flowing chords soothed my soul and touched my spirit. The next moment the Leslie vibrated as a wailing note brought us up from our seats in praise. Momentum built as the music rose into a Holy Ghost frenzy. The whole congregation exploded in worship, shouting, dancing, and praise!

Throughout this book you will read references to the "Hammond B-3" organ. In case you are one of the few who are unfamiliar with this instrument I will pause for a few moments to give you a brief history of this iconic musical wonder.

The Hammond first appeared in 1934 but the revered "Hammond sound" wasn't introduced until 20 years later. The first Hammond organ was sold to Henry Ford, inventor of the modern automobile. Common expressions such as *"pulling out all the stops"* was derived from the draw-bars of this popular instrument. The distinct sound of the classic Hammond B-3 organ and its Leslie rotary-speakers soon took the world by storm and it has since effected virtually every genre of music from Gospel, to Blues, to Jazz, to Rock and Roll. There have been many and varied attempts to emulate the instrument but none have managed to recreate it. Hammond B-3 organs which were manufactured between 1954 and 1975 are considered the Stradivarius' of the organ world and are in precious demand.

While there are many organists in existence, few of them them have the ability to master the Hammond B-3. There are organists and there are Hammond B-3 organists. Comparing a B-3 to a regular organ is like comparing the Stradivarius to a fiddle—there is no comparison.

The B-3 is a very *special* instrument with a very *special* sound that can only be played by *special* talent.

Joe Seymour is one of those who has mastered this very complex instrument. Yet he had no formal training in music—he simply prayed a prayer, sat at the organ, and as a great anointing came upon him, God miraculously guided his fingers and within one month various traveling evangelists were trying to persuade him to travel with their ministry.

His anointed talent opened doors for him to travel with some of the leading ministries in the United States. It is from these rich and varied experiences which much of the material of this book is drawn.

In this book you will also discover that Joe is more than an organist. He is also a minister and one which works in the gifts of the Spirit. There are no sugar coated words and feel-good phrases in his message. It is straight from the hip. He minces no words as he ministers that nothing but the blood can save and heal you. His ministry is one of the very few of the old time tent evangelistic ministries.

Newspaper headlines verify daily that prophecy is being fulfilled and that we indeed are living in the end-times. Jesus Christ is about to return.

"They shall see the Son of man coming in the clouds of heaven with power and great glory. And he shall send his angels with a great sound of a trumpet, and they shall gather together his elect from the four winds, from one end of heaven to the other" (Mat 24: 30,31).

May this book be a tool to stir it's readers to prepare for the final days of history which we are now entering. May it embolden you to return to old fashion revival.

But most of all, may it encourage you to stand in the gap.

—*Dr. Curtis D. Ward*

PREFACE

It was just an ordinary night when Joe Seymour lay down on his bed with a book propped up in his hands.

Little did he know that this night would forever change the destiny of both his life and ministry.

It was to effect not only his personal life but the lives of multitudes that would ultimately be drawn to his spirit filled ministry.

The book was about the ministry of William Marion Branham written by Gorden Lindsey. With intense interest he absorbed the stories of the supernatural miracles God had performed upon the people of that day. It was as though the anointing of God still permeated the pages and was imparting the same anointing into the depths of his very soul as he hungrily read it.

Late into the night he closed the book, got up and turned out the lights, and then laid back down again. He felt the need to talk to the Lord and began to fervently call out his name. As he prayed to God he felt the anointing from Heaven rain upon his soul in an unusually powerful way. As he lifted his left hand in prayer he felt a pressure and a warmth in the palm of his hand. He paid little attention to it as he continued in intense prayer.

Then suddenly he noticed something very strange . . . the pressure and the warmth was becoming more noticeable! It was becoming stronger and stronger with each breath he breathed!!!

It was then he looked up and to his utter astonishment saw HIS HAND WAS GLOWING!

A soft light was clinging to his hand like a celestial glove!

Joe closed his eyes and then opened them again. IT WAS STILL THERE!!! He slowly moved his hand in motion and the glow of the light followed it.

He closed his eyes and opened them again.

Sure enough it was still there.

Sometimes there appeared to be a visible flame of fire in palm of the glow. He realized something very unusual and significant was taking place but just wasn't sure what it was.

It was then the voice of the Lord began to talk to him. The voice told him that when he prayed for people that he was to use this left hand and the power of the Holy Ghost would move through it and the powers of hell would be thoroughly shaken by it!!! He was to never forget the voice that reverberated his whole being that night.

What God spoke to Joe Seymour at three o'clock in the morning on May fifteenth of two thousand seven has come to pass in powerful demonstrations of healings and miracles from God before crowds of witnesses.

Just when it seemed as though miracles were a thing of yesteryear God is, in these end times, restoring the ministry of supernatural gifts, signs, and wonders.

We have arrived at the threshold of the coming of the Lord. He is restoring a Bride of supernatural exploits and phenomena. You are invited to be a part of the last revival before Jesus comes.

This is YOUR revival, this is YOUR day, and this is YOUR hour. This is YOUR opportunity to stand in the Gap.

WHEN HE PRAYS, GOD HEARS HIM.

—Dr. Curtis D. Ward

CHAPTER ONE

STANDING IN THE GAP

If you are attempting to do anything for God you are standing in the gap. From the very beginning of human history God has always had a man or woman who was willing to step forward and stand in the gap for him. Some are well known and others are known only in the lambs book of life, but they all had one thing in common—they all stood where God placed them.

Moses stood in the gap for the children of Israel. *"The LORD said, I have surely seen the affliction of my people which are in Egypt, and have heard their cry by reason of their taskmasters; for I know their sorrows; and I am come down to deliver them out of the hand of the Egyptians, and to bring them up out of that land unto a good land and a large, unto a land flowing with milk and honey; unto a place of the Canaanites, and the Hittites, and the Amorites, and the Perizzites, and the Hivites, and the Jebusites."* (Exodus 3:7,8)

Where God guides, God provides. God moves in everything he puts together and just when it seems like something is going wrong—God steps in! Praise his name!

A lot of people in the present day church-world seem to think that the senior pastors, the assistant pastors, or even the evangelists, are the only ones that God has standing in the gap.

This is not true!

Every single person that was ever born was made to stand in the gap.

YOU were made to stand in the gap and if you do not take your rightful place, God will use whosoever is willing. If God has to use a sinner he will. In my many years of ministry I have had more sinners help me than children of God.

I once put a tent up in Columbus, Ohio and I informed several different preachers, pastors, and children of God that I needed assistance to do it. But I ended up having only three people show up and one was a complete sinner. The preachers and pastors failed to show up. *HOWEVER,* once all of the labor was done and the tent was up, they all showed up and wanted to preach under the tent.

THAT IS NOT STANDING IN THE GAP!

I could relate numerous examples like I have described above.

God *WILL* use sinners to help stand in the gap. Please don't misunderstand the point I am attempting to make, there *are* good preachers and children of God out there who are willing to step forward. What people need to really understand is that *you don't need to wait* for God to have you to do something. Jesus said, *"The harvest truly is plentiful, but the labourers are few; pray ye therefore the Lord of the harvest, that he will send forth labourers into his harvest.* (Matthew: 9- 37-38).

You are standing in the gap when you pray for someone.

You are standing in the gap when you visit someone in the hospital or nursing home

You are standing in the gap when you pray for someone that no longer has a family or family members to pray for them.

You are standing in the gap when you listen to someone who needs someone to talk to.

You are standing in the gap when you visit the shut in, the lonely, the forgotten, and you share with them, sing songs for them, pray for them, or just simply talk with them and brighten their day.

You are standing in the gap when you sing, teach, or preach.

There are many gaps that need someone to stand in. Find your place and ministry in God. Stand in the gap for someone.

That's my ministry —standing in the gap. What is yours?

You don't have to have a big name or big title— just stand in the gap for others.

The apostle John wrote, *"Whoso hath this world's good, and seeth his brother have need, and shutteth up his bowls of compassion from him, how dwelleth the love of God in him?"* (I John:3:17) It's not only goods, but also the needs.

Stand in the gap, and you will be putting your treasures in Heaven.

CHAPTER TWO

GOD ALWAYS HAS A RAM IN THE BUSH

No matter what God tells me to do, I have always done my very utmost to do it. I have always attempted to give him all that I have. There is nothing on this earth that belongs to me. I may have earthly things such as a home, an automobile, family, and other things. But God only lets us borrow these things . . . they really belong to God anyway.

But if God would ask us to sacrifice something *great*, would we be willing to do it? When the Lord spoke to Abraham and said to him *"Abraham: and he said, Behold, here I am. And he said, Take now thy son, thine only son Isaac, whom thou lovest, and get thee into the land of Moriah; and offer him there for a burnt offering upon one of the mountains which I will tell thee of"* (Gen. 22:2).

Abraham was willing to sacrifice his son. It must have been very difficult for him, yet he was willing to do it. *"And Abraham lifted up his eyes and looked and behold behind him a ram caught in a thicket by his horns: and Abraham went and took the ram and offered him up for a burnt offering instead of his son"* (verse 13).

Praise God!

Sometimes God will test us to see what we are willing do for him. But the Lord doesn't work one end without working on the other. He always has a ram in the bush.

God has tested me on numerous occasions. He once spoke to my spirit and told me to go to Mansfield, Ohio for a three day revival. It was the first time I had ever preached. Oh yes, I was nervous, but I had to go.

Before I left for the revival I was in a church where I was the organist. I was in the back making a sign for the three day meeting when the test began. The pastor of the church had had another evangelist in for a meeting. The pastor came back to the room where I was and ask me what I said to the evangelist to make him mad at her. I replied that I had not said anything to him and that I didn't know what she was talking about. This incident thoroughly upset me. I never had the slightest idea of what was going on. She said that the evangelist said that this was his last night there. But I had not seen him at all that day. I was beginning to get discouraged. I was *so* discouraged, I didn't want to go to Mansfield. So I went to another room to get away from everybody and started weeping. I didn't understand what was going on. I opened my Bible which fell open to a certain chapter and the Lord started to talk to me. I started to read that chapter and it was as though the very words were jumping out at me. I started reading and it began to feed my soul. Instead of saying "forget it" that I was not going to Mansfield, instead of leaving the church and going home, instead of letting my feelings get in the way of someone's blessings or my own blessings, I got my Bible and found a place to be alone with God. After I found the peace of the Lord I went back to my room and continued working on my sign.

Paul said, *"When I would do good, evil is present with me."* Isn't that the truth! We had a great meeting in Mansfield! Praise God! And in the end I discovered that the evangelist was mad at something the pastor did, not at me. The pastor was trying to pass it off on myself.

God will turn it around for you if you hang in there and have a little talk with him. God always has a ram in the bush. Read it and he will let you know he is working on both ends. He will not let you go through a test or a sacrifice unless he has an answer waiting for you on the other side. There are so many stories that I could tell you about and trials I went through, but the end result was that God always had a ram in the bush.

REMEMBER GOD *ALWAYS* HAS A RAM IN THE BUSH.

CHAPTER THREE

COVENANT WITH GOD

To have a relationship with God is the best thing we could ever accomplish. God made a covenant between himself and Abraham, "I *will make my covenant between me and thee and I will multiply thee exceedingly"* (Genesis 17:2).

I believe in the prophets of old. I also believe there is no respect of persons with God. I believe what God does for others he will do for you.

I was reading about Abraham one evening and God spoke to my spirit. He told me that I could make a covenant with him. I was instructed to get a sheet of paper and sit down and write what I expected him to do for me. So I did. Then he told me to write down what I would do *for him*. So I did. This was on May 20 of 1996.

There is nothing like making a covenant with God and it really works. The reason I know it really works is because most everything that I had written down that day has already come to pass and is still coming to pass.

God told Abraham *"It shall be a token of the covenant betwixt me and you"* (17:11). God told me that the token of the covenant between him and me is our word—and that is enough for me.

Make a covenant between God and yourself, and see if it doesn't work.

It will.

CHAPTER FOUR

GIFTS

When I first came into the church, it was like discovering a whole new world. The spirit of the Lord continually ministered to me. One night in a church service I saw a person playing the Hammond B-3 organ, and it touched my spirit within me in a great way. I prayed and asked God if he would teach me how to play the organ. This was in Columbus, Ohio down on South High Street at Sister Graves revival center. I hung around after church each evening and helped Brother Charles Graves clean the revival center after services. One night I asked Brother Graves if I could take care of cleaning the whole revival center by myself. He said that he could not pay me. I said, *"You don't have to pay me. Just let me sit down at the organ and practice playing it each night after I am through cleaning the church."* He was grateful because he drove a long distance to the revival center, so he gave me the O.K.

A great joy flooded through my soul.

Every night I would go to the church and make sure that the center was thoroughly cleaned up. Then I would go over to the organ and I would sit down and pray. I learned three cords and then I sang the song "Amazing Grace."

Before I knew it the Lord had placed his touch upon it. Before the month was over several evangelists ministered at the center and before they left they tried to persuade me to travel with them to play the organ. But I prayed and the Lord wouldn't allow me to go at that time. He had other plans for me. I thank God for that.

When God gives you a gift, he does not give it to you to sit on, but he gives it to you so that you can bless him and bless others. I am blessed every time I play the organ and I thank him continually. When God gives you a gift in music, in singing, in prophesying in tongues, or maybe in the word of knowledge, he expects you to use it. God has many gifts. He may give some people a gift in knowing how to build houses. He may give some people a gift in knowing how to work on cars. There are all kinds of diverse gifts. Use what he gives you and he will give you more. He has done so for me. (Read I Corinthians 12).

CHAPTER FIVE

SACKCLOTH

The Lord spoke to my spirit one evening and told me he wanted me to wear sackcloth. I didn't know what sackcloth was. I got my Bible out and I looked it up in the book of Isaiah. As I read this the spirit of the Lord came upon me and I knew he was talking to me.

I had a sackcloth made and I wore it for thirty days before I went to Atlanta, Georgia to preach in a meeting. The Lord blew me away. An explosive revival broke out and went non-stop for more than a month.

People were saved, healed, delivered, and miracles took place all around us. One lady was seeking the baptism of the Holy Ghost with the evidence of speaking in other tongues and the Lord gave me a word for her. He said to tell her when she rides back to the hotel with her sister, that her sister would receive the baptism of the Holy Ghost and that she would immediately begin speaking in tongues and that it would then move on over to her. It happened exactly as the Lord had revealed it would happen. The ladies then returned to the meeting and testified that the word had been accurate and that what I had prophesied *would* happen *had* actually happened.

God is great. God moves in many ways. That was one of the best meetings I have ever had. Why? Because I did what God told me to do and wore sackcloth. I didn't just wear sackcloth but I fasted and prayed also. The Lord told me to wear sackcloth only when he instructed me to, because when he did, miraculous things would begin to take place.

I was sixteen when I first received the Lord into my heart. Some people go to Bible school to learn the Bible and ministry but that was not the path God had chosen for me at that time. He had another path for me.

The church I went to in Columbus shut down. I then started to play the organ for various evangelical ministries. I played both for big name evangelists and small. I played for some of the largest ministries in the world, as well as smaller anointed ministries. I have learned a lot on the road with preachers I worked with. I worked with both good ones and bad ones (not knowing they were bad). Remember I had just given my heart to the Lord. I was still learning about the church. Please do not misunderstand me, there are many good preachers out there. But there are also some out there for the wrong reasons. One thing I did learn was that God keeps his hand on you when you are his child. The church is about salvation, love, peace, joy, and growing in the Lord. It is about giving him all the praises, helping people young and old, and teaching them the word. It is about doing the work of the Lord and carrying on where the disciples left off.

I have worked in churches, tents, auditoriums, and I have also taken my ministry to hospitals, nursing homes, and individuals homes preaching, praying, singing, and shouting. I have been blessed in everything I have done for the Lord Jesus.

The Lord Jesus told his disciples, *"For I was an hungred, and ye gave me meat: I was thirsty, and ye gave me drink: I was a stranger, and ye took me in: Naked, and ye clothed me: I was sick, and ye visited me: I was in prison, and ye came unto me.*

Then shall the righteous answer him, saying, Lord, when saw we thee an hungred, and fed thee? or thirsty, and gave thee drink? When saw we thee a stranger, and took thee in? or naked, and clothed thee? Or when saw we thee sick, or in prison, and came unto thee?

And the King shall answer and say unto them, Verily I say unto you, Inasmuch as ye have done it unto one of the least of these my brethren, ye have done it unto me." (Matt. 25:35-40)

That's what it is all about. I have learned a lot. My greatest schooling came from the Lord and from personal experience.

There are real preachers out there as well as the bad. Jesus said there would be wolves in sheep's clothing. I have always prayed and ask the Lord to not let me be like those preachers that are looking for life in the sand and to always be true to the Lord. He has always brought me through and he will bring you through also if you call upon him.

CHAPTER SIX

FAVOR

Sometimes God gives you favor with people. Sometimes he gives you favor with people of renown or someone who is a public icon. They are there at just the right time at the right place. God gave favor to David. It just started in a sheep field and he ended up King of Israel. God gave him favor with Saul (I Samuel 16-14). Look at Joseph and his brothers (Gen 37). They sold their brother Joseph and he went from the pit to the second in command next to the very Pharaoh himself.

God will give you favor with people. He has given me favor with individuals both great and small. Some were influential in worldly affairs, some were anointed men of God, and some had large ministries which opened many other doors for me. He gave me favor with people such as Reverend Leroy Jenkins, the renowned television evangelist, whom I played the Hammond B-3 organ for. I played the Hammond B-3 for Evangelist Tony Leyva and preached under his large cathedral tent in Atlanta Georgia. One tent revival with Tony lasted more than 30 days. I played the B-3 Hammond organ for Evangelist Roy Young for 3 yrs and traveled with him under his gospel tent. I also was the organist in his church. Other ministries I have been associated with include: Evangelist Don Young, Pastor Charles and Helen Graves of Graves Auditorium, Evangelist Dorothy Davis, Reverend David Jones (Evangelist Thea Jones' son), Dr. Curtis Ward (Evangelist and pastor), and Evangelist Edward Adkins. Most of my spiritual growth, however, was nurtured under the anointed ministry of Reverend Charles Young, Sr., my spiritual daddy and pastor.

I played the Porta-B Hammond organ with Tony Toliver during a tent revival (He was the keyboard player and back-up singer for the singer Dottie West). I often filled in for Bobby Floyd at a church in Columbus. Floyd toured with Ray Charles for three years and also played the B-3 with other nationally known artists. I played the organ with Gene Walker (renowned saxophone player who played for Aretha Franklin, Billy Joel, the Beatles, and many others). I also worked with organist Charles Solomon. Bob Dorsey, who played the drums for country star Tom T. Hall, played the piano for me.

I also played for Redd Stewart, the country music star and television entertainer.

Do you remember Flippo the clown on television? Flippo, whose real name was Bob Marvin, was the host of the early show in the 70's. I grew up watching him on TV. I got to know him through my friend Dale Durthaler, owner of Durthaler's Organs and Pianos. Marvin promoted his pianos and organs on TV.

One day I shared with Dale that I grew up on Flippo and Dale told me that he came in the store sometimes wanting to go to lunch. I told Dale that I would like to meet him. Dale told me that the next time he came in that he would call me and we would go out to lunch. Two weeks went by and then Dale called me. *"What are you doing?"* he asked. *"Nothing,"* I replied. Dale said, *"Come down to the store. Flippo is on his way we are going to lunch."* We went to Red Lobster on Hamilton road.

Bob Marvin was just as funny in person as he was on TV. He had me laughing in stitches. And that was how I first became acquainted with him. He was a really great person but he has since gone on to his reward.

I was privileged to work in revival services with Ronald Coyne. When Ronald Coyne was a little 7 year old boy in Oklahoma he lost his right eye while playing with a piece of wire. Because of infection his eyeball was surgically removed. He was fitted with a plastic eye to replace his real eye. Obviously he was totally blind in that eye.

An evangelist called him out during a revival

meeting and prayed for him. He began to be able to miraculously see from an eye which was not even there.

Local papers picked up the story and soon skeptical reporters were at his doorstep to test his miracle eye. Sometimes they tested him with his parents out of the room and with his good eye securely covered . To their surprise he could read anything they gave him to read and he could identify objects. Reporter after reporter tried to fool him and doctor after doctor tested him.

He grew up to be a mighty man of God traveling the world and proving to all that the same God that healed the blind man at the gate could heal a one-eyed man from Oklahoma. Ronnie traveled widely demonstrating this ability to audiences around the world and giving all the glory to Jesus. He appeared before large groups, and guested on T.V. shows such as 'That's Incredible.'

In his revival services he would ask for a couple of volunteers to assist him in proving that his was blind. He had them bind up the right side of his face with a bunch of gauze and adhesive tape so that no vision or any light at all could penetrate through to his good eye. Then he popped his glass eye out of the other eye-socket and held the eyelid open so that everybody got a good look at the empty socket. He would walk down the aisle, allowing you to peer directly into the empty hole. He then requested volunteers in the audience to give him anything they wanted him to read. He correctly read peoples social security numbers from their cards and even their drivers license—all through the empty socket where there was no eyeball.

One man relates that Ronald spoke to his father during a service and said, *"If you would hand me the Bible where you opened it there."*

He then gazed at the page through the empty eye-socket and out loud he read, *"This is in Matthew 15:14 and it says 'Let them alone: they be blind leaders of the blind. And if the blind lead the blind, both shall fall into the ditch.'"*

As this book is being prepared to go to print I am preparing for a tent revival with Jack Coe, Jr.

Jack Coe Jr. is said to have been especially close to his father, Jack Coe Sr., who was one of the most prominent television evangelists and tent revivalists of the 1940's and early 50's. He was widely known for having some of the largest healing revivals that took place in that era. His huge crusades were conducted underneath one of the largest gospel tents in the world. Thousands were healed of all kinds of sicknesses, diseases and afflictions and to this very day he is remembered as the boldest healing evangelist of the 20th century.

Jack Coe Jr. stepped into his fathers shoes and began his own ministry after the death of his father. Today he ministers through television, church, and tent ministry. Thousands have been saved and healed under his ministry.

To me, it is a divine gift to be able to have favor with such great men of God who have roots in such a wonderful, godly heritage.

God has given me grace with people from many different walks of life.

God will give you favor and the opportunity to meet people. He will give you the opportunity to testify to them about the Lord and what he has done for you.

But the greatest favor of all was the blessed day that Jesus forgave you of all your sins.

Now THAT is divine favor!

Joe played for "Redd" Stewart, country music star and television entertainer, who was inducted into the Nashville songwriters hall of fame in 1970.

Joe Seymour (on the right) with television evangelist Leroy Jenkins (left).

Bobby Floyd (left) played for such personalities as Ray Charles and Diana Warwick. Bobby traveled with Ray Charles for three years.

Joe with Gene Walker (left), renowned saxophone player for personalities such as Aretha Franklin, Billy Joel, the Beatles and many others.

Charles Solomon (right) has played the organ for large ministries such as David Epley Ministries in Miami.

Joe with Annie McRay (left), gospel singer.

Charles Young, Jr. (on the right).

Donny Young (right), television evangelist .

Sharon Burton (on the right) poses with evangelist Seymour after her miraculous healing. Doctors were unable to find any trace of the previous illness in her body.

Tony Toliver (right) posing with the author.

From left to right: The author, Joe Holbrook (from Channel 10 News), Mrs. Holbrook, and television personality "Fritz the Night Owl."

The Seymour family. Top left to right: Mary, Earl Sr (Joe's father), and Earl Jr. Second row: John, Tiny (family pet), Joe (the author), Mike, Louise (Joe's mother), and Gloria (below).

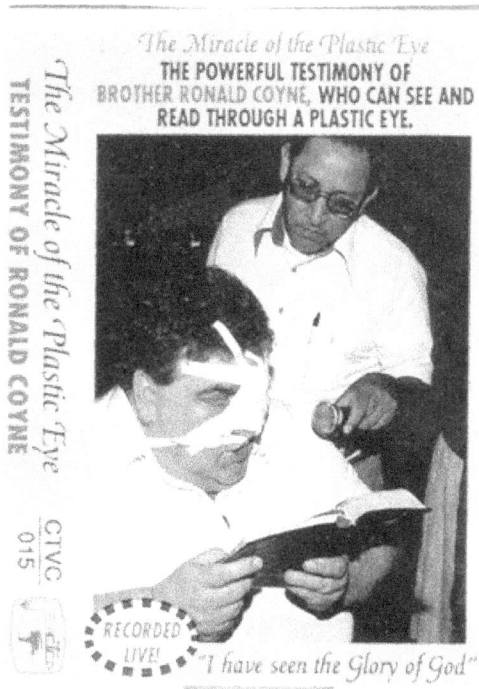

A flyer advertising the Ronald Coyne ministry.

A flyer advertising the Jack Coe Jr ministry.

Joe Seymour playing the Hammond B-3 organ.

Joe Seymour preaching the Word.

Joe Seymour ministering to the people.

The author praying for the sick.

31

The sawdust trail!

Joe Seymour Ministries.

CHAPTER SEVEN

THE CHURCH

W hen I was growing up as a kid life was great.

I had a good family. My Dad would get up everyday and get a cup of coffee, sit down at his desk, and get his Bible out. He would read it and start typing on his old typewriter and before the day was done he had created stacks of paper filled with notes and scriptures. He was a scholar in the Bible. If you asked him a question he could tell you where, when, how, and what they were doing. He was very well versed in the scriptures.

Mom and Dad taught us right from wrong. They raised us up in the admonition of the Lord, to fear him as well as love him, because he first loved us. We didn't fear him because he was bad. We were taught we only need fear him when he was upset with *us* for being bad.

We often had prayer meetings in the house. Dad would teach and people would go home and come back again and again because they were hungry for the word. It wasn't like it is today when it seems as though people don't fear God anymore. They act like he owes them. The church has changed so much since those days and church people seem to be continually changing. Just when I think that I have heard it all, someone comes up with something ridiculously new. The churches today fight over everything possible, from communion to pre or post tribulation. Do they not understand that people are going to believe what they want to believe anyway?

Why? Because that's the way Satan wants it. That is why there are different churches out on every street corner. They are divided. They are not one church working together. The word instructs us that as a body of believers we are many members but one body. Yet we have ended up with so many churches out there that we have confused people beyond measure. That's why they say, *"I don't know what church to go to."* If we confuse people as we do, don't you think that we are confused about what *we* think? That's why Jesus said he was coming after a church without spot, wrinkle, or any such thing.

Wake up people!

Many have even twisted up the doctrine of their very salvation. For example, some people believe that once saved always saved. If that was true why would he say in Hebrews 10:26 *"For if we sin willfully after that we have received the knowledge of truth there remaineth no more sacrifice for sin?"* Wake up people! Sin is what destroyed the earth in Noah's day. Did they not all go to hell . . . all but Noah and his family? (Genesis 6:1). Read it. There is only one Word (John 1:1) and one Church, and not one million different churches. His word will stand when this earth is destroyed. People don't want to hear this, but the truth will set you free.

If all the members would come together as one body and quit trying to prove who is right, we could have great revival. If we allow the Holy Ghost to lead us, he will teach and guide us into all the truth. There is but one word—not many words—but one word of God. The churches preach so many different doctrines and their main doctrine is *"If you don't believe like I do, you will go to Hell."* Well, it's not your word, it is *his* word, and in the end *he* gets all the praise.

His true word will inspire you. His true word will guide you. His true word will heal you, deliver you, and keep you when the storms come.

Many people simply won't do anything for God unless they get the credit.

They are not standing in the gap.

They complain and cry about everything.

Jack Coe Sr. said that the modern church

meetings are like having tea parties—cold as ice from the pulpits to the pews. They are having social clubs and do not even blush to bring everything abominable into the church. They are leaving God out and setting him aside *until* they need him. Then when he doesn't answer them they say *"I wonder why God let that happen?"*

When I look back at the day of A.A. Allen or William Branham and view their films, tapes, and books, I wonder what happened to the church and the people who worked with these pioneers of yesteryear. Why didn't they carry on the spirit of revival they ignited in that day? A.A. Allen had some of the most miraculous healings ever to be medically recorded. He paid a price for what had happened in his tent crusades and in the establishing of Miracle Valley. People devoured it but they didn't allow it to sustain them.

Those who were part of these revivals should have carried the power of the Holy Ghost onward so that it would be spread all over the world. But when Allen died, people fought over who would carry his mantle or take over his ministry. It was as though when Allen died, that particular revival died. But the revival was not Allen's— it was Gods. People shouted for the moment but failed in the momentum.

Try to prove me wrong and I'll show you I'm right.

What happened to the church? People are looking for another revival they believe God is suppose to send and they say that it will begin in the church. How can that be if the church is out there sinning like everybody else.

When I said it died when Allen and Branham died, I was referring to "right now" miracles, healings, and deliverance . . . "right now," no waiting for it, documented reports.

Whose reports are you going to believe . . . not only in society but in the church?

"Be ye followers of me as I also am of Christ. Now I praise you, brethren, that ye remember me in all things, and keep the ordinances, as I delivered them to you. But I would have you know, that the head of every man is Christ; and the head of the woman is the man; and the head of Christ is God" (I Corinthians 11: 1-3). We are to follow Paul as Paul followed Christ. We are commanded to obey the ordinances of God, the law of God, or the statutes. But many people have it backwards. The woman tells the man what to do or else he is out of his house. They usually don't even have to divorce because they weren't even married in the first place.

The church today calls evil good and good evil, along with the world. Read Isaiah 5:20. There are two churches in this world—the worldly church and the church of God. I am not talking about the churches on every corner with that name above their door, but I am referring to THE church of God. Preachers and pastors got away from the law of God and the ordinances of God. Why? Because this is a modern day—if it feels good do it.

Things have changed and we have changed with them. The music in many churches has even taken on a worldly sound. Some of the music in todays churches would cause Allen, Branham, and Coe to shake in their very graves.

The old time preaching praying, singing, shouting, and even holiness, seems to be outdated in todays modern churches.

We didn't need changes. If the changes were so necessary and were made to make a difference, then *why* are we not seeing, miracles healing, deliverance, and salvation like we did back then?

The only time you see these kind of miracles today is when you go out of the country. You don't see that today in America like they did in the days of Allen, Branham, Wigglesworth, and McPherson.

God help us. We are running from it. We don't want to pay the price, so we all go back to our churches and argue over the word and about which one of us is right. I'm not trying to tear down the body, or hurt the body, I just want to stir the church to get closer to God.

We can do more for him if we wake from our slumber. How can we see souls saved if we don't want to pay a price and get hold of God? If we don't have the desire, how can we have revival?

We need to read more of the word, fast more often, and pray a little longer.

Sin is the problem. We don't want to give it up. How can we expect to make the rapture if we have sin in our life? Allen once told the story about going into his secret closet. In the confines of that dark place the Lord told him that there were 13 sinful things he had to get out of his life before he could have the power that he wanted. After that experience the power followed his ministry.

When they heard these things why didn't the people who worked with him find a closet and pray and fast until *they too* heard from God? If they had given their all, then we would now be going to *their* meetings watching *them* do the work of Jesus . . . and when we in turn worked with them we could learn and go do what they were doing. But somebody somewhere dropped the ball.

Smith Wigglesworth said we need to get sin out of our lives so that we can be more like Jesus. I have heard people (even pastors and preachers) say were not perfect and were not holy. That's because they don't want to be. We sing the song "to be like Jesus, to be like Jesus, that's all I ask is to be like him" while in reality we don't want to. *"Be ye therefore perfect, even as your father which is in heaven is perfect"* (Matthew 5:48). *"Sanctify yourselves therefore, and be ye holy: for I am the Lord your God"* (Leviticus 20:7).

Preachers and pastors will tell you what God will do *for* you, but won't tell you *what* you have to do to get it. Proverbs 13:18 says, *"Poverty and shame shall be to him that refuseth instruction: but he that regardeth reproof shall be honoured, time and time and time again."*

The word tells us to clean up our act but we refuse to do so, because we let our flesh override us. You might say, *"Brother Seymour, it sounds like you are very hard with what you believe."* No, the word has always been there to instruct us and to keep us in line. Why do you think that God told Noah to build the ark. Genesis 6 :8-9 tells us that *"Noah found grace in the eyes of the Lord. these are the generations of Noah: Noah was a JUST MAN*

AND PERFECT IN HIS GENERATION, AND NOAH WALKED WITH GOD." That is the way the church is supposed to walk.

Hezekiah said, *"I beseech thee, O Lord, remember now how I have walked before thee in truth and with a perfect heart, and have done that which is good in thy sight. And Hezekiah wept sore"* (II Kings 20:3).

Paul wrote, *"Having therefore these promises, dearly beloved, let us cleanse ourselves from all filthiness of the flesh and spirit, perfecting holiness in the fear of God."* (II Corinthians 7 :1).

CHAPTER EIGHT

AN INSANE ASYLUM WITHOUT WALLS

The world is an insane asylum without walls. We live in a world that has no boundary's because we, as a society, believe that we are good people. Yet we hear daily of world events occurring that is of an insane nature, even in our own county.

There are many people which you think are of a sound mind, which suddenly do something utterly insane. Even your own neighbors will surprise you with their dysfunctional view about life, religion, and politics.

Oh, yes . . . politics.

Who's, who, what brand are you . . . Democrat or Republican?

Who are you really? A pawn in someones hands that lives in the asylum? Oh yes, the asylum. When people can't get things done, who do they trust? They murder people, rape people, misuse, hurt people, control, and corrupt people. They criticize people and stir racial prejudice.

The media especially damages lives and fills our minds with negative material.

We fight amongst one another. And when the fighting subsides, we are only resting, gathering strength to fight again.

It started in Genesis chapter 3, subsided in Genesis 6, and returned with a vengeance in Noah's day and it continues to this very day.

But in the midst of all of mans insane confusion, Jesus Christ came on the scene. He became our Emmanuel—God with us.

What we fail to understand is that the world is dead . . . even to God. Why? Because Jesus said in Matthew 4:4 *"It is written, man shall not live by bread alone, but by every word that proceedeth out of the mouth of God."*

His word is life eternal. Amen.

People say, *"Well, Jesus came into my life and if I fall he will pick me up again."*

Yes, he will, but when you give your heart and your burdens to the Lord he will carry you through. You must understand that Jesus shed his blood for you so when you do sin he will forgive you but *he also gave you power to live a sinless and godly life*. Thats where we fail to understand.

The Lord said it best when he said, *"My people are destroyed for lack of knowledge: because thou has rejected knowledge, I will also reject thee, that thou shalt be no priest to me. Seeing thou hast forgotten the law of thy God, I will also forget thy children"* (Hosea: 4 – 6).

Yes, we have grace but when we break the laws of our father in heaven, but *we must quit sin* or we will not enter into heaven.

The Bible is full of instruction. There is no reason for us not to know what sin is and what it isn't. With the Holy Spirit within us we have the power to bring ourselves under subjection.

But most of us just don't want to.

We bring things upon ourselves because of sin in our lives. I'm not any better then anyone else, but everyday I work on bringing my flesh under subjection.

We read in the Bible of great men and women who faced great obstacles but were able to overcome. We read about those who gave their lives for the cause of Christ.

We read of others who gave their all. We read about those I spoke of earlier such as Smith Wigglesworth, A.A. Allen, William Branham, G.T. Haywood, William Seymour, and those who gave all they had and lived for God.

But the greatest example of all was when the Lord himself became man and was tempted in all points the same as we are, but yielded not to temptation.

But who are we to say it can't be done.

But our so-called church world, or may I say the worldly church, promotes the attitude of *"live however you want and do whatever you want to do and you are still saved."*

Saved means forgiven to sin no more.

No more.

You know them by the fruits they bare.

Most of those in the modern church do not know the laws of God, or if they know them they willingly break them.

Its like an insane asylum. Pastors and evangelists break them even in church. Their wives don't dress appropriately before getting on the platform, wearing tight pants or dressing worldly. I know you are calling me a clothesline preacher because most people resort to name calling to justify their wrong. They don't admit, and can't admit, they are wrong because their wives run their home also.

44

How do I know? I worked with many of them. Some of them lined up to the word of God. Many did not. Paul tells us how the church should operate but many just turn a deaf ear. They justify everything. They would rather waver, listen to others and avoid *their* wrath than to avoid the Lords wrath.

Hear me now!

The sanctuary should be holy and true.

I was putting my tent up for a revival when the Lord began to speak to me. He told me to don't let anybody on the platform during that revival. I asked him where were the singers supposed to sing. He told me to place a rug and a mike stand on the ground in front of the platform and let them stand there. So I did. He told me to keep the platform for his word to be spoken from. But oh how it made the people angry when I told them! Some walked out and some stayed. It was from these actions that I knew who had the power of stick-ability for God.

I am old school . . . because it works for me in everything I do.

CHAPTER NINE

SPIRIT WORLD

As a kid growing up I had the privilege of being reared by a loving caring, family, who was interested in helping other people. We also had the privilege of just being kids.

When I was 13 yrs old I remember my mother was laying on the couch and I heard her talking to someone. I got up and went into the front room.

"Mom, who are you talking to ?" I asked.

"Doty," she replied.

Doty was our cousin (my mother's sister's girl). Doty was confined to a wheel chair. Mom said that she saw Doty standing there, reaching her arms out to her, and then suddenly she disappeared.

We didn't have a telephone, so the lady down the street came to our house the next morning and knocked on the door with a message for us. My mother answered the door and the lady said that somebody wanted to talk to her on the phone. Mom went to the lady's house and when she came back she had a funny look on her face.

"Mom, what is wrong?" I asked her.

She said, *"Doty passed away last night."*

You could have knocked her down with a feather . . . and me, as well!.

My mother infrequently had some other experiences like this.

If people would be truthful they have had strange supernatural experiences themselves.

When I was a kid I had unexplainable experiences but I never shared them with anyone.

But around 2005 strange things began to happen in my life.

I lived in Galena, Ohio in a small farmhouse. I liked it there. It was a very quiet and serene place. One evening I was watching the news and fell asleep on the couch.

I woke up.

It was dark outside and I saw that my kitchen light was on. I saw a woman standing there as clear as you would look in the mirror and see yourself. She was that real.

She was over 4 feet tall and wore a dress like they wore back in the 50s' or 60s'. She had dark hair. I could only see half of her. It look like she was doing something in the kitchen. She was standing halfway in the door way.

Three days later I saw two women in the kitchen (too bad I couldn't get them to stay and cook me some good 'ole country food . . . you know how much I love to eat).

Three days later I saw a man in my music room. He had a navy coat on and blue jeans. He was looking down at my drums and had his back towards me. At the same time I saw a girl standing in the corner of the room. She was about 13 to 14 years old with long brown hair. She was just staring at me.

It would be some time before I would understand the nature of these unsettling experiences.

Another strange visitation occurred while I was living at the south-end of Columbus. I was sitting in a Lazy Boy recliner in the front room. I was lying back in it and fell asleep. My Hammond organ was next to my chair.

When I woke up I was facing my organ. I saw a little girl on my organ bench looking dead-set in my eyes and acting like she was playing my organ. She was very pretty and was wearing a black Paris hat and a pretty dress.

When I saw her I jump out of my chair, looked at her, and then she was gone.

She startled me.

But the Lord was revealing to me that I would soon meet someone who needed instruction.

And sure enough, it soon came to pass.

In one church I was going on stage where there were long curtains behind me. My brother John, my friend Danny, and myself were there playing music. I quite playing music and I went to other side of the stage. I heard my moms voice say, *"Joe."* I knew it was her voice. I stopped and heard the voice two more times.

I asked my brother if he said something and he said, *"No."*

I asked my friend if it was him and he replied, *"No."*

I was just trying to avoid the voice. But hearing that voice made me pay attention and to be careful of what I said and did that evening. A situation arose that could have caused much confusion. As a result I was spared of saying the wrong thing at the wrong time.

There was a time that I was at my daughters house. Two weeks before, I asked God, *"Why is it that I can only see people at night why can't I see them during the day time?"* Well I should have not said that. After that I fell asleep, during the day, on the couch. When I woke up there was a little girl standing in front of the coffee table. Her back was towards me and she had brown hair. She was about 7or 8 years old. At the same time I saw a man at the end of the big couch. Then they disappeared.

I was not afraid in the least, but I felt calm and peace.

These were real . . . I could see them.

I wondered what these strange experiences were. Were they angels manifesting in the form of people? Were they visions? Were they symbolic or were they actual?

I know the Spirit of the Lord and I have the gift of discernment and I have never felt anything demonic during these experiences.

These various manifestations appeared for a reason. I am not at liberty to explain the exact meaning of these visitations at this time but perhaps, if God permits me, I can elaborate on them in another book. Suffice it to say that anything God shows you will ultimately have a purpose.

For example one morning I woke up early about 6 or 7 A.M. I looked up towards the ceiling and there in the midst of the air was an arm from the shoulder down to the fingers. There were keys in his hand and he was shaking them.

After this my ministry broke forth in mighty revival! It was as if some mighty force had "unlocked the door" to my ministry using the keys to the kingdom.

Some reading this will immediately get spooky and think, *"Ghost."*

Well, thats not true. God can send visions or angels and if we are not spiritually minded we will not get the message he is trying to give to us.

God can open doors for people but if they don't walk through them it's their own fault.

There are things that God wants to show us but how can he if we're afraid.

When you let God show you things in the spirit, no matter what it is, God will speak to you. Don't let people take it from you. There is a meaning for everything which the Lord shows you in the spirit world.

Don't listen to people. They will say its Satan, "Oh stay away from them." Well, if that is the case, then visions are a thing of the past. Everything that Jesus did, they said he was of the devil. They condemned the prophets also.

Wake up.

There is a difference between what Satan sends you and what God sends you. You will know by the word and by the Spirit. *"Beloved, believe not every spirit, but try the spirits whether they are of God; because many false prophets are gone out into the world"* (I John: 4)

But don't be afraid to enter the spiritual realm. If God is with you, the devil can't touch you!

CHAPTER TEN

THE ANGEL OF THE LORD

One afternoon I was walking from my RV to the gospel tent across the lot and an angel appeared walking about 20 feet in front of me. He was young and in a white robe. He was reading. It looked like he had a book in his hands. He walked by me and then disappeared into thin air.

Little did I know that something very incredible was about to take place during the service that evening.

I was wearing a sackcloth robe during my sermon

that night. A man that I knew attended the service. He had a cancer as big as a baseball which was growing on his chest. The Lord told me to call him out for prayer, and so I did.

The man informed me that he had to go often to the Ohio State University hospital for dialysis. As I laid hands upon him and began to pray, the presence of the Lord began to move and we both knew that something remarkable had just taken place.

A week went by and the man came to the tent again.

He stood up during the service and excitedly testified that God had totally healed him!

When he showed me his chest where the tumor had once been I was ready to shout!

The tumor was completely gone!

In addition to that, he never again needed dialysis!

Praise God!

Back in the 90's, the Lord spoke to me about erecting my 40 by 60 canvas gospel tent in Lancaster, Ohio. I located a lot at route 22 and route 37 and rented it. My brother John and a few of our friends put the tent up and soon we were in revival services.

The Lord began to use me in a great way and God was miraculously touching peoples lives.

One evening a man came under the tent and sat in the second row with his wife. He never spoke a word. He never gave me any indication that he was a Christan. He just sat there.

When I was through preaching, I felt a great anointing come upon me, much greater than that which I had been preaching under. For a moment I was unable to move as the warmth of this anointing flooded over me.

I suddenly became aware that somebody was standing by my right side.

I managed to look to my right.

No one was there!

I again looked toward the audience, but again I was strongly aware that someone was standing by me. I could not see the person but I could feel a presence there.

It was then I realized . . . it was the angel of the Lord!

To my amazement the angel began to speak to me.

The angel instructed me to call that man in the second row out of the audience.

"What is going on here," I thought to myself.

The voice spoke to me again and said even louder, *"Call that man out of the audience."*

His voice caused me to literally tremble

I feared that if I did not obey that the voice would get even louder, so I spoke up, *"Sir could I pray for you?"*

It was then that I saw a spotlight shine down upon the man.

It was like a heavenly, otherworldly glow that descended upon him.

Then the voice instructed me to call out his wife.

I thought to myself, *"What if its not his wife. It could be his sister or friend."*

So I said, *"Mame, are you his wife?"*

"Yes," she answered.

"Would you stand beside your husband?" I instructed her.

She arose, and stood beside her husband, and as she did that same heavenly, glowing spotlight came upon her.

I thought to myself, *"Whoever is talking to you told you she is his wife, and I feel the sweet presence of the Lord giving me assurance. I know the presence of the Lord and this is certainly his presence."* So after that I started listening to the voice and have never stopped listening.

I told the man and woman some things that night that I had no way of knowing. There was one thing in particular that the man wanted to hear from God—I told him that the Lord told me that he was called to preach.

After that you could have knock him down with a feather.

He testified afterwards that he was going through a hard trial and that he was ready to give up preaching. He said that he had asked God, *"If that preacher on the platform is a man of God, reveal to him that I am called to preach and let him tell me."*

Do you see what I am saying? There are all kinds of things God will do if you let him.

Many times I have been ministering when I suddenly realize that someone is standing on my right side and then he begins to speak to me.

God also anoints hand towels I carry with me as I minister under the anointing. When I'm done preaching I begin to minister to people and the Lord will tell me to give the towel to someone in the audience. They usually come back and testify that God gave them a miracle.

I was working with my brother in Crestline Ohio at a cemetery years ago in the 70's. He was in charge of all the business at the cemetery.

We were digging monument holes for the concrete man so he could fill them. My brother was above me digging and I was digging below.

Then I felt the presence of the angel of the Lord beside me.

I looked up by the road and there was a friend of mine looking at a lot which had not yet been dug. He was not there in reality . . . I was beholding a vision.

In this vision I saw him looking down into the grave.

I looked to see who was in the grave and it was his mother.

In reality the woman I saw in the grave was actually in the hospital. The hospital told her they didn't have the proper equipment to work on her so they would have to fly her to the Ohio State University hospital.

But she didn't want to fly.

The next day I went to the fire station to see my friend and I asked him how his mother was doing.

He said, "S*he's up cussing the doctor out so I guess she's doing OK.*"

I told my brother Mike what I saw and he thought I was nuts. I told Mike that she is going to die and I told him the exact place where they would bury her.

At this point he *really* thought I was nuts.

The next day we were working and one of his board members wanted to see him. When Mike got back I was at his house drinking coffee.

He told me that my friends mother had just passed away. He then informed me that they were going to bury her in Galion Ohio.

I just looked at him didn't say a word.

My faith in what I had seen was firm. I knew what I saw and stayed with it. When God shows you visions and dreams, or takes you somewhere in the spirit . . . if you are certain it is from God, then stay firm with it.

The next day his board member wanted to see him after work. I went home, got a shower and afterwards went to Mikes house. I was sitting on his couch watching TV and Mike came in, sat down in a chair, and was staring at me.

I looked over and asked, *"Whats wrong?"*

"How do you do that?" he replied.

"How do I do what? I responded

"Well, their not going to bury her in Galion Ohio," he said, *"They are going to bury exactly where you said. How do you do that?"*

"Mike I just don't do that. God does that," I said.

Sometimes I have visions. Sometimes I have dreams. Sometimes I see manifestations of angels. I don't do anything . . . it just happens. There is much more I could share with you but I'll save it for another book in the not-to-distant future.

You don't know how far God will take you if you let him. God is a wonderful father. Remember, Psalms

46:1 *"God is our refuge and strength, a very present help in trouble."*

He will help you through everything. He has always been there for me.

One evening I was holding services in an auditorium when I suddenly became aware again of the presence of the angel beside of me. The angel of the Lord was showing me names written in the midst of the air. These were names of people that I didnt know, but the people I was praying for *DID* know them!

As we were interceding for them some jumped to their feet with testimony's of miracles and deliverance. People were receiving healings and miracles.

In the middle of the service the angel of the Lord told me to pray for a certain lady in the crowd. The angel was instructing me exactly what to say in my prayer. I prayed that the Lord would give her the house she wanted and to send an angel of the Lord with her. I further told her that when she went to court that things would go in her favor and also that God would give her a car.

When I got through praying she said, *"How did you know all of this I was going through?"*

She was going to court the next morning.

When I'm in a meeting and ministering to the people the angel of the Lord is there moving through the auditorium and anything can happen.

During one service the angel of the Lord even spoke to me about someone in the audience which was going to be facing the angel of death. Soon afterwards they passed away.

Around 2006 I was in a meeting with another evangelist when a man began screaming under the influence of demonic possession. His actions terrified the whole church. We laid our hands on his head and the demonic activity became worse. It took over four hours to cast those demons out. But today that man is free and is still serving the Lord!

In 1998 I was in the UCT auditorium building holding a great meeting. The place was packed out. I prayed for a lady whose doctor diagnosed a bump on her face as cancer. In the midst of the Holy Ghost moving mightily upon me I told that cancer to dry up and die.

The woman came back to the services two days later and testified that the cancer was gone!

You could see it was no longer there!

Her doctor was amazed!

This is one of many healings that took place.

I have been blessed to witness great miracles and healings. I have been blessed to witness the greatest miracle of all . . . sinners set free and covered by the blood of Jesus! There is nothing greater than leading a soul to Christ and see them fall on their knees at the alter in repentance. There is nothing greater than to see lives changed and transformed.

I have experienced many trials and many valleys, but the angel of the Lord was with me every step of the way. I have ministered to both small and great . . . both the rich and the poor. God has sent to me those who were hurting, abused and searching for answers. Many were stumbling blindly in the bleakness of the night through dark valleys which they were humanly unable to cross. In those crucial hours God sent them to me for one purpose and for one purpose alone . . . to stand in the gap for them.

I want to encourage you, no matter what talents you may have or what talents you may lack, to simply use what you have, and go boldly into the fields which are ripe. Time is short. Work while it is yet day. In these last hours of human history, as the final curtain begins to fall, may the glorious return of the Lord find you standing in the gap.

Finis

You may order CD's and DVD's of the authors organ playing and preaching from the following address:

Joe Seymour
P.O. Box 271
Westerville, Ohio,
43086

JoeSeymour1@yahoo.com

You may visit the author at the following web sites:

PastorJoeSeymour.com

JoeSeymourMinistries.wordpress.com

www.GospelTent.us

AtriaBookPublishing@gmail.com

www.ingramcontent.com/pod-product-compliance
Lightning Source LLC
Chambersburg PA
CBHW051850040426

42447CB00006B/779